Space Mysteries

Mysteries of Stars

T0386294

Margaret J. Goldstein

Lerner Publications ◆ Minneapolis

Lerner Publications Company
An imprint of Lerner Publishing Group, Inc.
241 First Avenue North
Minneapolis, MN 55401 USA

For reading levels and more information, look up this title at www.lernerbooks.com.

Main body text set in Adrianna Regular 14/20.
Typeface provided by Chank.

Designer: Mary Ross

Library of Congress Cataloging-in-Publication Data

Names: Goldstein, Margaret J., author.
Title: Mysteries of stars / Margaret J. Goldstein.
Other titles: Searchlight books. Space mysteries.
Description: Minneapolis : Lerner Publications, [2021] | Series: Searchlight books - space mysteries | Includes bibliographical references and index. | Audience: Ages 8–11 | Audience: Grades 4–6 | Summary: "How do stars form? What are they made of? Find out in this high-interest STEM title that introduces young readers to the mysteries scientists are currently exploring about stars"— Provided by publisher.
Identifiers: LCCN 2019049930 (print) | LCCN 2019049931 (ebook) | ISBN 9781541597389 (library binding) | ISBN 9781728413884 (paperback) | ISBN 9781728400891 (ebook)
Subjects: LCSH: Stars—Juvenile literature.
Classification: LCC QB801.7 .G648 2021 (print) | LCC QB801.7 (ebook) | DDC 523.8—dc23

LC record available at https://lccn.loc.gov/2019049930
LC ebook record available at https://lccn.loc.gov/2019049931

Manufactured in the United States of America
1-47842-48282-2/13/2020

Contents

Chapter 1

STAR POWER

Red giants, white dwarfs, pulsars, supernovas, and even the sun—the names are different, but all these things are types of stars. A star is a hot ball of gas that makes enormous amounts of energy.

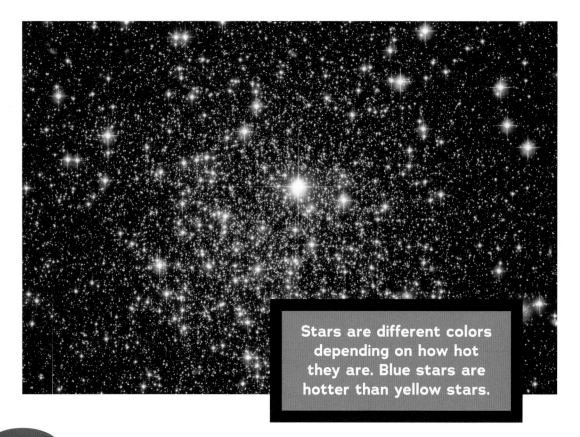

Stars are different colors depending on how hot they are. Blue stars are hotter than yellow stars.

It takes about eight minutes for the light from the sun to reach Earth.

The sun is the closest star to Earth. Every second, the sun produces enough energy to heat all the buildings and run all the machines on Earth for five hundred thousand years. Some stars make even more power. A star called Rigel produces forty thousand times as much energy as the sun.

OUR SOLAR SYSTEM HAS EIGHT PLANETS.

▼

Our Home Star

Astronomers can learn a lot about stars by studying our home star, the sun. The sun is the center of our solar system. The planets and their moons, millions of asteroids, and trillions of comets all travel around the sun.

Like most stars, the sun is made mostly of hydrogen and helium, plus small amounts of other materials. The center of the sun, called the core, is extremely hot and dense. This is where bits of hydrogen smash together to create energy. The energy travels from the core, through the sun, into the sun's atmosphere, and then into space. Most of the sun's energy is made of light and heat.

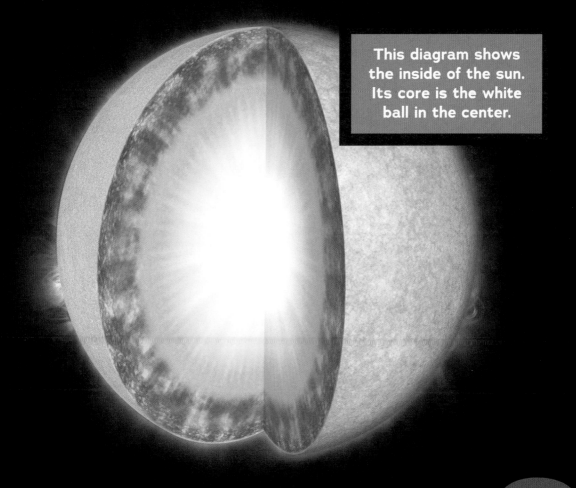

This diagram shows the inside of the sun. Its core is the white ball in the center.

The sun is an action-packed place. During solar flares, the sun's atmosphere erupts with light. During coronal mass ejections, the outer layer of the sun's atmosphere, the corona, shoots large clouds of gas into space.

Material from a coronal mass ejection can travel at 2.2 million miles (3.6 million km) per hour.

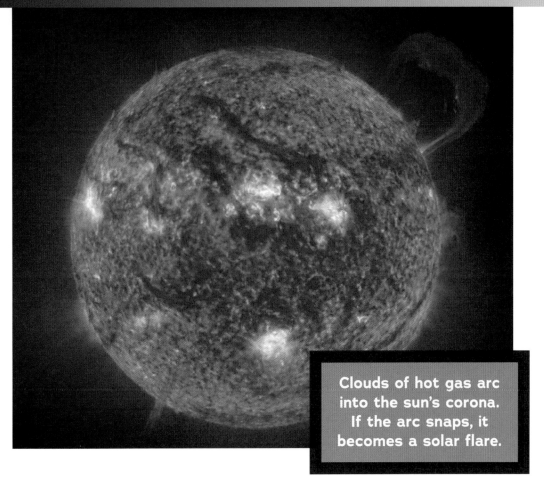

Clouds of hot gas arc into the sun's corona. If the arc snaps, it becomes a solar flare.

The Sun's Mysteries

Scientists want to learn more about the sun. They want to study the solar wind. This high-speed wind carries particles from the sun to the farthest edges of the solar system. Particles from the solar wind, solar flares, and coronal mass ejections sometimes hit Earth's atmosphere. When they do, they can harm space vehicles and electrical equipment. Scientists are figuring out how to predict this "space weather" so they can reduce the damage.

WHEN THE MOON BLOCKS THE SUN'S LIGHT, WE CAN SEE THE CORONA.

▼

Scientists also want to learn more about the corona. It is much hotter than parts of the sun that are closer to the core. Scientists don't know why.

STEM Spotlight

The *Parker Solar Probe* took off from Earth on August 12, 2018. During its mission, the probe will make twenty-four trips around the sun.

When *Parker* gets close to the sun, the temperature outside is nearly 2,500°F (1,371°C). A thick shield protects the probe and its instruments from burning up.

The probe uses its instruments to study the solar wind, space weather, and the corona. It also carries cameras for taking pictures. The data *Parker* collects will help scientists learn more about the corona and space weather.

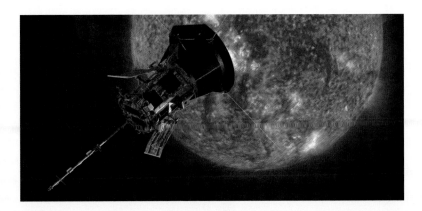

Chapter 2

FAMILIES OF STARS

Young stars form inside giant clouds of gas and dust called nebulae. The gas and dust clump together and begin to spin. The clump grows as gravity pulls in more gas and dust. The clump spins more quickly and gets hotter. When it gets hot enough, the bits of hydrogen inside start smashing together to create energy. The clump becomes a star. Sometimes a disk of gas and dust swirls around a new star. This material might break apart to form planets.

The Lobster Nebula is about 5,500 light-years away from Earth. It is full of new stars.

YOU CAN SEE THE PLEIADES WITHOUT A TELESCOPE ON A CLEAR NIGHT.

Some nebulae make thousands or even millions of stars. In a star cluster, all the stars were born around the same time. They move as a group through space. Gravity holds them together. One famous star cluster is the Pleiades, or the Seven Sisters. Ancient astronomers named this cluster for its seven brightest stars. But the Pleiades actually contains hundreds of stars.

Many galaxies are
shaped like spirals.
Some galaxies look
more like blobs.

Outcasts

Galaxies are groups of billions of stars, all held together
by gravity. Galaxies also contain planets, moons,
comets, asteroids, nebulae, and other space objects.

But not all stars belong to galaxies. Many stars travel in the space between galaxies. Astronomers think these stars used to be part of galaxies. But galaxies sometimes collide. The energy from a collision can fling stars out of their galaxies. In 1997, the Hubble Space Telescope found hundreds of stars between distant galaxies. Some scientists think that half of all stars in the universe might be in between galaxies.

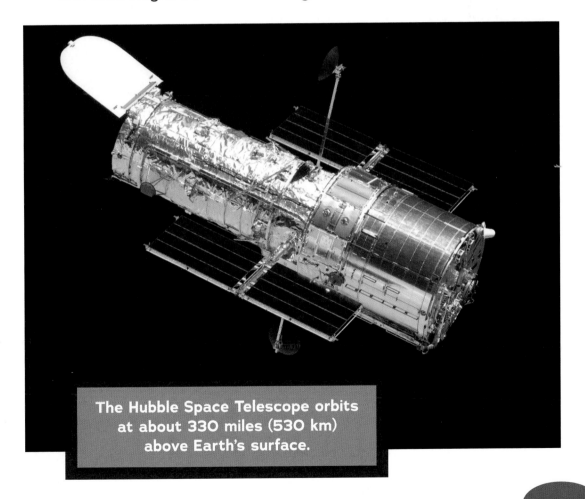

The Hubble Space Telescope orbits at about 330 miles (530 km) above Earth's surface.

This illustration shows the edge of a planet (*lower left*) that orbits two stars.

Two Suns in the Sky

Our solar system has one star. But there are many solar systems besides our own. Some have two or more stars at the center. In fact, astronomers think that more than half the solar systems in our galaxy have more than one star. Astronomers have found a faraway exoplanet in a solar system with two stars. If you lived on this planet, called Kepler-16b, you would see two sunrises and two sunsets every day.

STEM Spotlight

Scientists think the first stars that ever existed contained only hydrogen, helium, and lithium. As the stars made energy, they created new materials, such as carbon, oxygen, and iron.

Even though these stars died long ago, their light might still be traveling through space. Scientists in Europe think they have found some of this light. The light seems to have come from stars made only of hydrogen, helium, and small amounts of lithium—the ingredients in the very first stars.

Chapter 3

END OF THE LINE

Stars have different life cycles depending on their mass. Low-mass stars can live for billions or trillions of years. High-mass stars last only about 100 million years. Stars that are between high-mass and low-mass stars burn for millions or billions of years. The sun is one of these stars. It has been around for about 4.6 billion years.

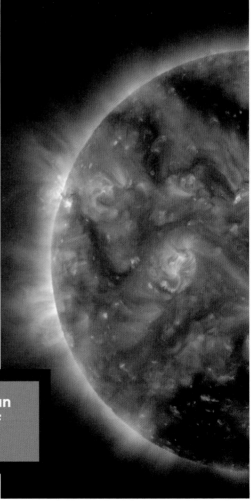

Scientists think the sun will live for a total of ten billion years.

The Hubble Space Telescope photographed this supernova in another galaxy.

Low-mass and intermediate-mass stars end their lives quietly. They use up all their hydrogen and cool down. Eventually, their outer layers blow away into space. But high-mass stars end life with a bang. They explode and shoot gas and dust far out into space. An exploding star is called a supernova. The light from a supernova is billions of times brighter than the sun.

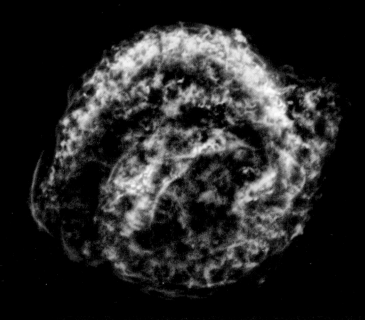

After Kepler's supernova exploded, it left behind a cloud of dust and gas. Modern astronomers use telescopes to study this cloud.

Flash in the Pan

In 1604, German astronomer Johannes Kepler saw a bright object in the sky. He didn't have a telescope. He saw the object with just his eyes. He called it a stella nova, which means "new star."

Later astronomers figured out that the object wasn't a new star. It was an exploding star. Astronomers coined the term *supernova* in the 1930s.

Kepler was the last person to observe a supernova with the naked eye. Modern astronomers use powerful telescopes to watch supernovas.

Space Fact or fiction?

Humans and stars are made of the same materials.

This is true. As famous American astronomer Carl Sagan explained, the materials in our bodies, such as the calcium in our bones and the iron in our blood, were originally formed inside stars. When the earliest stars exploded as supernovas, these materials spread out into space. Some of them ended up in nebulae. New stars and planets formed inside nebulae. One of these planets was Earth, and the material from stars became the building blocks of life.

Chapter 4

SUPERSTARS

After a high-mass star explodes, the core usually remains behind. If the core is less than three times the mass of the sun, it becomes a neutron star. Neutron stars are small and dense and spin very quickly. They are only about 12 miles (20 km) across. But they are packed with more material than the sun.

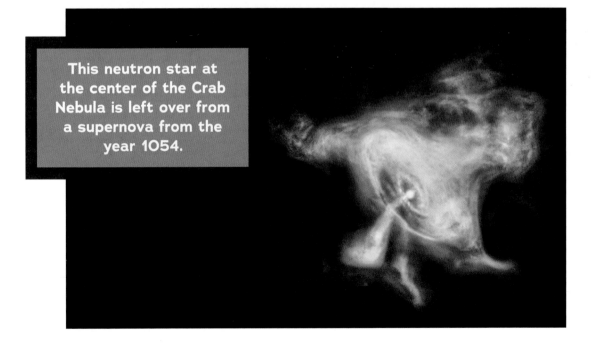

This neutron star at the center of the Crab Nebula is left over from a supernova from the year 1054.

SOME NEUTRON STARS LET OUT BEAMS OF LIGHT FROM THEIR POLES.

▼

Inside a neutron star, powerful forces produce beams of radiation, such as radio waves. In 1967, Jocelyn Bell was studying astronomy at Cambridge University in England. Using a radio telescope, Bell picked up a radio signal from space. The signal pulsed once every 1.3 seconds. Most radio signals from space don't have a pattern. But this one did. Bell and her teacher wondered if aliens were sending the signals. After doing more research, Bell realized that the signals were coming from a neutron star.

As a pulsar rotates, it sends out a beam of light that sweeps past Earth at a steady rate.

Starstruck

Since 1967, scientists have identified different kinds of neutron stars. Those that send out radio signals in a pattern are called pulsars. Those that send signals with no pattern are called rotating radio transients. Astronomers are working to find out why some neutron stars send out signals in patterns and others do not.

Magnetars are neutron stars with superpowerful magnetic forces. Sometimes these forces cause powerful X-rays and gamma rays to burst from the magnetar. Astronomers call this a starquake. They are studying magnetars to learn what causes starquakes.

Astronomers have a lot more to learn about neutron stars. They want to know what goes on inside them. They also want to learn more about the X-rays and other radiation from neutron stars.

A magnetar's magnetic field is millions of times stronger than those of machine-made magnets.

From Star to Black Hole

A black hole is a region of space with so much gravity that nothing can escape. A black hole might form when a high-mass star explodes as a supernova. The outer layers of the star shoot off into space. But the star's core does not become a neutron star. It collapses into a tiny point and becomes a black hole.

Most galaxies have huge black holes in their centers.

Black holes are invisible because their powerful gravity traps light. Astronomers do not know what happens inside a black hole. They can't study black holes using optical telescopes. But they can take pictures of stars circling around the edges of black holes. They can also measure energy coming from objects swirling around black holes. In 2019, astronomers used radio telescopes to make a picture of a black hole at the center of the galaxy called Messier 87.

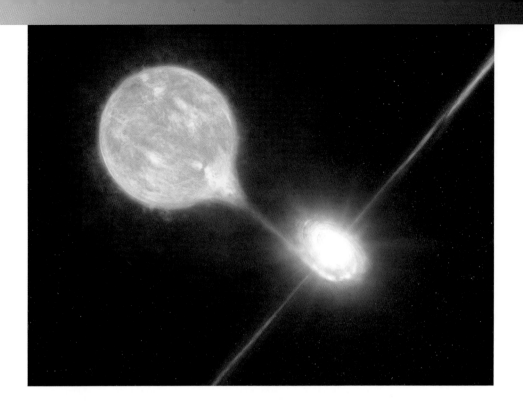

THIS ILLUSTRATION SHOWS GASES FROM A STAR SWIRLING INTO A BLACK HOLE.

Black holes sometimes let out huge jets made of gas. Astronomers want to know how black holes make these jets, so they study the jets using the Chandra X-ray Observatory. This space telescope can detect X-rays. The James Webb Space Telescope will launch into space in 2021. This powerful telescope could detect other kinds of energy coming from black holes. These telescopes will also tell us more about the mysteries of other kinds of stars.

3D Printer Activity

The Chandra X-ray Observatory is on a mission to detect X-rays coming from supernovas, black holes, and distant galaxies. To download instructions for making a 3D-printed model of the observatory, visit the below link.

PAGE PLUS

https://qrs.lernerbooks.com/Chandra-Xray

Glossary

astronomer: a scientist who studies objects in space

atmosphere: a layer of gases surrounding a planet, star, or other object in space

comet: an object made of ice, rock, and dust that travels around a star

corona: the outer layer of the sun's atmosphere

dense: containing matter that is packed together extremely tightly

exoplanet: a planet outside our solar system

gravity: an invisible force that attracts objects to one another

mass: the amount of matter in a star, planet, or other object

optical telescope: a telescope that gathers visible light coming from space

radiation: energy, such as light, that travels in waves

radio telescope: a telescope that gathers radio waves coming from space

Learn More about Stars

Books

Kurtz, Kevin. *Cutting-Edge Black Holes Research*. Minneapolis: Lerner Publications, 2020.
Black holes are invisible, but by studying energy coming from black holes, scientists have learned a lot about these powerful regions of space.

Peterson, Christy. *Breakthroughs in Stars Research*. Minneapolis: Lerner Publications, 2019.
Learn about our sun, other stars, and how astronomers are unraveling their mysteries.

Simon, Seymour. *The Sun*. New York: HarperCollins, 2015.
The closest star to Earth is our own sun. By studying the sun, scientists can learn about other stars in the universe.

Websites

Space Place
https://spaceplace.nasa.gov/search/stars/
This site from the U.S. National Aeronautics and Space Administration offers information on the sun, supernovas, nebulae, galaxies, and other topics related to stars.

The Sun
https://kids.nationalgeographic.com/explore/space/sun/
National Geographic Kids provides fun facts about the sun, with links to other space topics.

Supernovas
https://www.esa.int/kids/en/learn/Our_Universe/Stars_and_galaxies/Supernovas
Learn about supernovas at this site from the European Space Agency. You'll also find links to more information about stars and galaxies.

Index

Photo Acknowledgments

Image credits: ESA/Hubble & NASA (CC BY 4.0), p. 4; ESO/M. Kornmesser (CC BY 4.0), p. 5; DETLEV VAN RAVENSWAAY/Science Photo Library /Getty Images, p. 6; MARK GARLICK/ Science Photo Library/Getty Images, p. 7; NASA/GSFC/SOHO/ESA (CC BY 2.0), p. 8; ESA/ NASA/SOHO, p. 9; NASA/Aubrey Gemignani, p. 10; NASA/Johns Hopkins APL/Steve Gribben, p. 11; NASA, ESA and Jesœs Maz Apellÿniz (Instituto de astrofsica de Andaluca, Spain). Acknowledgement: Davide De Martin (ESA/Hubble), p. 12; NASA, ESA, AURA/Caltech, Palomar Observatory, p. 13; NASA, ESA, A. Riess (STScI/JHU), L. Macri (Texas A&M University), and Hubble Heritage Team (STScI/AURA), p. 14; Ruffnax (Crew of STS-125)/NASA, p. 15; NASA/ JPL-Caltech/T. Pyle, p. 16; NASA, H. Ford (JHU), G. Illingworth (USCS/LO), M. Clampin (STScI), G. Hartig (STScI), the ACS Science Team, and ESA. p. 17; NASA/Goddard/SDO, p. 18; NASA/ ESA, The Hubble Key Project Team and The High-Z Supernova Search Team, p. 19; Chandra X-ray Observatory Center/Smithsonian Institution/flickr, pp. 20, 22; ESO/VISTA/J. Emerson. Acknowledgment: Cambridge Astronomical Survey Unit (CC BY 4.0), p. 21; NASA/JPL-Caltech, pp. 23, 24, 25; ESO/WFI (visible); MPIfR/ESO/APEX/A.Weiss et al. (microwave); NASA/CXC/ CfA/R.Kraft et al. (X-ray) (CC BY 4.0), p. 26; Event Horizon Telescope Collaboration (CC BY 3.0), p. 27; ESO/L. Cal (CC BY 4.0), p. 28; NASA/Image courtesy of TRW, p. 29.

Cover: ESO (CC BY 4.0).